I'm Still F*cking Bored

Activity Book

For Adults

Featuring 100 Fucking Adult Activities: Coloring, Sudoku, Dot-to-Dot, Word Searches, Mazes, Fallen Phrases, Math Logic, Word Tiles, Spot the Difference, Where the Fuck did the Other Half Go, Nanograms, Brick-by-Fucking-Brick, Word Scramble, and Much More!

Thank you for your purchase, assholes!!
I hope you enjoy this goddamn book!

Please leave a review on Amazon and check out
my fucking awesome Amazon collection!

tamaraadamsauthor@gmail.com

Contact me to get a free printable PDF of activities at:
http://www.tamaraladamsauthor.com/free-printable-activity-book-pdf/

http://www.amazon.com/T.L.-Adams/e/B00YSROGC4

www.tamaraladamsauthor.com

https://twitter.com/@TamaraLAdams

https://www.facebook.com/TamaraLAdamsAuthor/

https://www.pinterest.com/tamara-l-adams-author/

Fucking a-MAZE-ing! Start at the top and find your way through this twisted pile of fuck.

Answer on page 102

Seeing double? Well wipe that shit out of your eyes, because there are 9 differences between these cocksuckers. Fucking find them! Answer on page 102

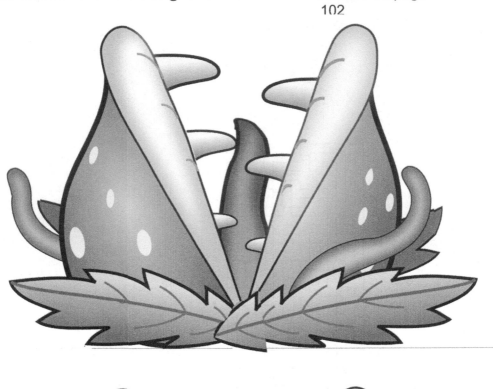

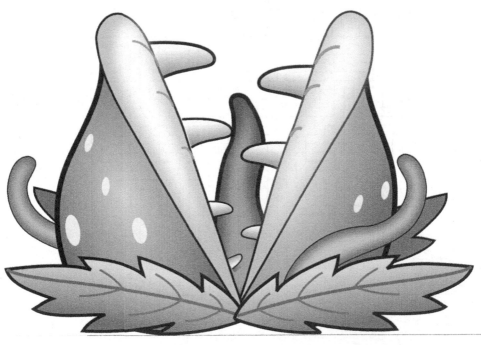

Here's a list of words to expand your vocabulary. See if you can pull them out of this shitpile of letters.

Fucker	Jizzstain	Ass
Pisswizard	Cuntpuddle	Dickweasel
Fannyflaps	Twatface	Fucknugget
Crap	Arsehole	Dickhead
Slut	Shitmagnet	Bitch

Answer on page
102

```
                              N  B  C
                           O  B  E  R  E
                           Y  M  S  A  D
                           B  J  O  P  O
                           F  I  P  F  M
                           P  L  T  J  S
                           V  C  O  C  D
                           P  U  T  U  H
                           F  N  L  J  K
                           J  T  E  I  O
                           U  P  W  S  Y
                           W  U  L  M  T
                           J  D  A  D  J
                           R  D  H  W  H
                           V  L  M  J  V
                           R  E  I  K  B
                           O  F  T  W  S
                        T  P  O  T     T  U  P  L  E
              M  C  E  P     I  L  J  M  O  R  U  D  N
P  U  R  S        C  M  L  O  S  F  D  W  V  N  L  T  M  E  I
S  A  S  S        Z  Q  G  S  N  I  D  Y  M  O  U  K  F  S  V
X  B  U  M  L  J  H  W  D  S  R  Y  I  Z  L  N  B  U  O  P
B  W  U  Q  W  C  I  G  J  R  V  W  T  C  C  O  P  G  P  F
T  T  E  S  X  Z  P  M  J  H  P  D  J  L  K  W  X  X  G  J
P  F  Z  X  A  R  Y  I  K  H  U  S  I  C  H  W  K  L  O  F
V  P  I  R  L  O  F  T  W  T  S  O  Z  R  S  O  E  P  T  U
D  M  D  C  L  T  U  O  R  J  P  P  Z  H  X  B  N  A  L  J
A  T  C  M  L  O  C  F  D  E  A  K  S  V  P  T  I  U  S  R           R  E  Y  U
E  D  K  H  F  S  K  C  O  P  L  O  T  T  Y  T  E  S  X  E  U  O  P  F  U  W  R
H  H  W  T  U  O  E  K  W  X  F  C  A  O  P  F  S  E  N  K  L  D  Y  X  W  J  O
K  C  L  J  S  P  R  H  S  K  Y  I  I  F  V  P  M  J  H  X  C  O  I  I  D  R  P
C  D  D  W  T  G  J  M  B  R  N  X  N  M  R  Y  I  K  H  K  B  C  U  P  O  V  B
I  B  E  W  I  Z  U  V  W  S  N  E  U  V  O  F  T  T  E  G  G  U  N  K  C  U  F
D  U  X  C  T  S  W  P  L  M  A  H  S  M  P  U  B  L  I  P  W  L  O  N  H  V
G  C  O  P  A  R  E  D  N  L  F  E  M  N  B  D  O  S  O  U  G  B  V  V
C  I  E  O  C  F  N  G  F  D  W  B  O  I  U  H  E  X  S  N  I  Y
S  K  P  L  T  Z  T  N  J  N  V  X  I  M  E  G  D  I  V  X
X  B  S  H  I  T  M  A  G  N  E  T  I  S  B  C  P  Y  T
   V  X  Q  B  R  V  H  W  B  V  C  R  H  U  K  M  P
      E  S  X  V  P  M  J  T  P  A  P  L  N  B
```

Assuming your ass can count, connect the dots from 100 to 140. All the other numbers are there just to fuck up your day!

Answer on page 102

258
218 268 278 240 276
101 102 243
147 233 233 244
144 248 264 245
238 223 104 103 249 242 238 146
246 105 106 237
254 245 243 250 237
257 253 272
251 255 107 274 247 239
254 108
265 279 141 236
270 226 254 275 164
271 166
100 110 109 248 185 249
262 230 168 167 246
264 258 259 236
238 250 265
256 241 169
112 113 116 117 257 272 150
242 269 239 212 243 266
241 152 214 160 247 269
259 239 210 267
244 253 171 256 170 241
239 222 262 239 260
155 114 115 195
237 268
237 236 259 226 261 172 250 245 143
236 196 263
268 225 111 119 118 271 142
235 211 174
239 277 197 263
212 275 236
217 121 198 122 188 175 240
235 266 210 173
207 209 261 236 248 176 177
279 278
215 213 271 123 187 178
145 124 199 186 181 179
214 189 273 260 180
234 238 276 126 184 183 182
228 151 217 125 200
260 264 206 269 275 194 213
263 215
278 256 120 128 127 267 237 249
277 216 218 209 193
270 220 261 274 246 252
227 247 266 130 131 133 252
262 279 237 190 224 134 274
158 238 228 202
225
234 224 252 244 242 132 135 149 251
227 191
272 148 205 231 211
257 216 270 255 220
267 258 138 229
153 204 229 253 273
129 140 139 137 136 222
251 154 276 203
159

4

Ever play Sudoku? I bet your sorry ass hasn't!
These are the goddamn rules.   Answer on page 102

Numbers from 1 to 9 are inserted into sets that have 9 x 9 = 81 squares in whole. Every number can be used just once in every 3x3 block, column and row, so don't reuse that shit.

- Every number can be used just once in the blocks of 3 x 3 = 9 square blocks. Use a number more than once, you fuck everything up.
- Each row of 9 numbers ought to contain all digits 1 through 9 in any order, so don't fucking miss any.
- Every column of 9 numbers should comprise all digits 1 through 9 in any order. Hope you can fucking count.

Here's a hint for your stupid ass: One way to figure out which numbers can go in each space is to use "process of elimination" by checking to see which other numbers are already included within each square – remember, no duplicates.

					6		4	8
		1	9		5			
6		7	2					1
							5	9
1		9	5		3	4		7
5	6							
7					2	3		4
			3		4	6		
3	2		8					

Number Blocks

Answer on page 102

Try to fill in the missing numbers if you can, asshole!

The missing numbers are integers (that means it's a whole number) from 0 to 9.
The numbers in each row add up to the totals to the right.
The numbers in each column add up to the totals along the bottom. Numbers can be repeated, so don't get fucked!
The diagonal lines also add up the totals to the right. Good fucking luck! Complicated? Fuck yeah, it's complicated!

				28
1	3			15
		7	0	17
	7		3	14
8		2		24
16	22	14	18	17

Who fucked these words up? Goddammit, now you have your work cut out for you. Unscramble each of the words to reveal your new motto.

Answer on page 103

Jstu

hsut

yrou

fucngik

mh.uto

I

no'td

akte

yan

hts,i

reev

nad

ml'

ont

ndoig

hits

oaydt.

Letter Tiles

Answer on page 103

This shit is fucked!

Move the jacked-up tiles around to make the correct fucking phrase.

The three letters on each tile must stay the fuck together and in the given order, so don't try to cheat, bitch!

RRY	WH	RE	LRE	EW.	I'M
OUR	HOU	T Y	YO	UPI	EL I
HUR	ALL	KN	FE	D I	ST
SO	Y T	NGS	ALL	EN	I C
I	ADY	YOU	U A	GHT	ED

I'M				

How many fucking words make up the goddamn giant fist?

Answer on page 103

Solve this bitch of a maze. Each finger is a separate maze to navigate, so it's really five fucking mazes in one. Ain't that a kick in the cunt!

Answer on page 103

This picture's fucked! Draw each image to its corresponding square to unfuckify it.

A1

A2

A4

B1

B2

B3

B4

C1

C2

C3

C4

D1

D2

D3

D4

	A	B	C	D
1				
2				
3	Leave A3 Blank			
4				

Image on page 103

11

One fucking asshole always has to stand out in a crowd. Find
the jerk that's different from the rest. Answer on page 103

Aw yeah, a FUCKING CRYPTOGRAM!

You are given a shit piece of text where each letter is substituted with a irrelevant damn number and you need to fucking decide which letters in the alphabet are being coded by the numbers you are given.

You need to use logic to crack this shit, so pull your head outta your ass and throw on your thinking cap, Sherlock.

Answer on page 103

A	B	C	D	E	F	G	H	I

J	K	L	M	N	O	P	Q	R

S	T	U	V	W	X	Y	Z
							7

__14__   __5__ __11__ __9__ __11__ __22__

__22__ __11__ __2__ __8__ __14__ __7(Z)__ __11__   __23__ __4__ __20__

__13__ __16__ __15__ __23__   __14__   __24__ __20__ __11__ __2__ __22__

__16__ __5__ __26__ __14__ __8__   __14__ '   __13__   __14__ __5__

__2__   __24__ __14__ __26__ __16__ __2__ __26__ __14__ __4__ __5__

__20__ __23__ __11__ __22__ __11__   __14__   __15__ __2__ __5__ '   __26__

13

Fallen Phrases

Answer on page 103

A fallen phrase is a fucked puzzle where all the letters have fallen to the bottom. They got jacked up on their way down, but remain in the same column. Complete this horse shit by filling the letters in the column they fall under. You start by filling in the one-letter columns, because those clearly don't have anywhere else to go in their column.

Don't make this shit harder than it has to be.

Also try filling in common one-, two- and three-letter words. I even gave your lucky ass an example.

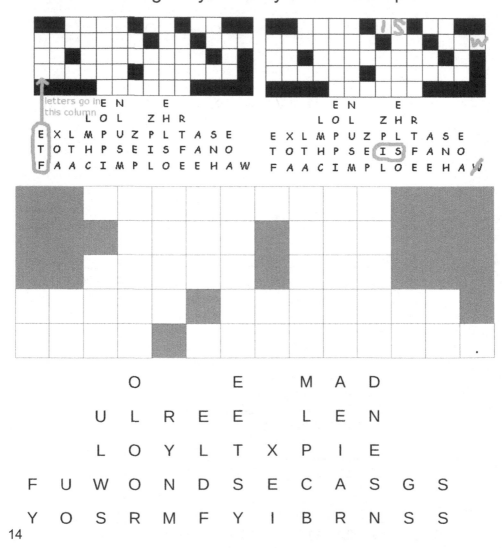

I can't read these fucking words. Unscramble the goddamn letters to create a shit phrase.

Answer on page 103

ml'

ont

giltiunns

uoy.

'ml

nsibdciger

oyu.

Oyu

esilmrabe

peeci

fo

hsti

orf

bins!ar

Color your ass off!

Balls! That's a lot of letters. Find the words in this cock.

Answer on page 104

Cockwomble   Douche   Bumblefuck

Bollockface   Fuck   Shitnubbie

Cumbubble   Shit   Fucktrumpet

Thundercunt   Asswipe   Douchecanoe

```
                    E  D  N  L  T  Y  M
                    N  G  F  D  W  C  O
              Z  Q  F  U  C  K  X  Y  M
              J  H  F  D  S  R  T  I  J
              R  V  H  J  B  I  C  F  H
              V  P  M  J  H  P  C  P  L
              R  Y  I  S  H  F  S  V  C
              O  F  T  W  T  U  O  P  R
              T  U  O  L  J  G  P  F  H
              O  G  F  D  W  X  G  J  M
              J  L  M  E  W  S  Z  U  V
              W  U  V  X  I  O  S  W  P
              Z  E  P  I  W  S  S  A  H
              J  H  F  D  S  Q  W  R  V
              R  V  H  J  B  S  X  V  P
              V  P  M  J  H  X  S  R  Y
              R  Y  I  K  H  K  L  O  B
              O  F  T  W  T  C  E  U  U
              T  U  O  L  J  M  M  O  G
              O  G  F  D  W  B  N  J  L
              J  N  V  X  L  M  H  J  K
              D  G  R  E  I  J  L  N  B
              J  B  F  C  F  II C  O  P
        E  S  X  V     J  U  P  C  P  L  R  W  X        J  O  P  R
     F  H  X  S  R  Y     C  H  F  S  V  C  H  J  K        O  F  P  F  H  X
  R  E  I  K  L  O  F  K  W  T  U  O  P  T  E  P  M  U  R  T  K  C  U  F  R
T  L  M  L  C  E  T  U  O  L  J  G  P  F  H  X  B  N  M  L  J  O  F  T  Y  T  G
V  S  E  C  B  L  O  G  F  D  W  X  G  J  M  B  V  X  Q  W  R  T  U  O  P  F  P
P  Y  I  K  H  M  S  V  C  O  P  T  H  U  N  D  E  R  C  U  N  T  F  F  E  P  D
Y  F  T  W  T  U  O  P  R  W  X  P  T  U  O  P  F  I  X  S  R  J  L  L  R  Y  O
F  U  O  L  J  G  P  W  H  J  K  E  O  G  F  V  P  M  B  H  X  W  B  V  O  F  U
U  G  F  D  W  X  G  J  K  B  F  R  J  L  M  R  Y  I  K  B  K  B  S  M  P  U  C
G  L  M  E  W  S  Z  U  V  C  S  P  W  U  V  O  F  T  W  T  U  Y  M  N  B  D  H
L  U  V  X  I  O  B  O  L  L  O  C  K  F  A  C  E  B  E  B  P  N  O  I  U  T  E
U  G  J  O  P  U  R  E  D  N  L  C  Y  M  N  B  D  H  M  O  P  B  T  X  E  O  S
Q  C  X  E  O  P  L  N  G  F  D  W  C  O  I  U  T  U  X  B  N  E  S  I  P  L  L
E  S  D  O  U  C  H  E  C  A  N  O  E  Y  M  P  C  D  B  V  X  E  X  B  H  M  E
   X  B  N  M  L  J  H  F  D  S  R  Y  I  J  B  C  O  Y  T  E  N  B  V  X  S
   B  V  X  Q  W  R  V  H                    P  F  H  I  Y  T  E  E
      T  E  S  X  V  P                       P  I  O  P  F  H
```

The fucking goal here is to fill the black boxes in the grid.

The numbers given on the side and top of the grid indicate the numbers of consecutive black boxes in each line or column. Got that, bitches?

Here's a goddamn example: 3,3 on the left of a line indicates that there is, from left to right, a block of 3 black boxes then a block of 3 black boxes on this line. Have I lost your ass yet?
To solve the puzzle, you need to determine which cells will be black and which will be fucking empty. Determining which cells are to be left empty (called spaces) is as important as determining which to fill (called boxes). Later in the solving process, the spaces help determine where a clue (continuing block of boxes and a number in the legend) may spread. Solvers usually use a dot or a cross to mark cells they are certain are spaces.

It is also important never to fucking guess. Only cells that can be determined by damn logic should be filled. An example is shown here:

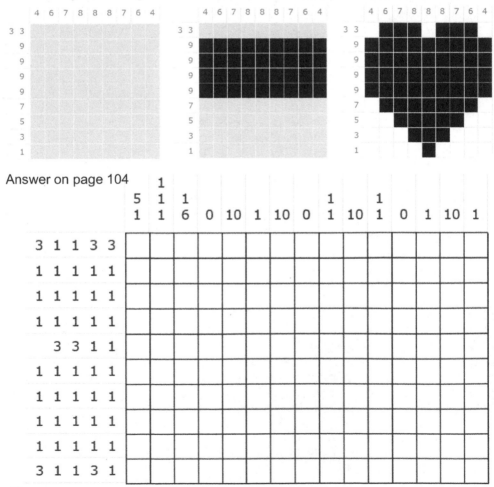

Answer on page 104

18

Answer on page 104

Try to fill in the missing numbers if you can, bitch!

The missing numbers are integers (that means it's a fucking whole number) from 0 to 9.
The numbers in each row add up to the totals to the right. The numbers in each column add up to the totals along the bottom. Numbers can be repeated, so don't get fucking confused! Keep it simple, stupid.
The diagonal lines also add up the totals to the right. Good fucking luck! Complicated? Fuck yeah, it's complicated!

				24
	4	6	8	20
7	2	5		23
4			3	15
		3		16
16	23	14	21	5

Seeing double? Well wipe that shit out of your eyes, because there are 11 differences between these cocksuckers. Fucking find them.

Answer on page 104

Assuming your ass can count, connect the dots from 100 to 137. All the other numbers are there just to fuck up your day.

Answer on page 104

230

218   258   278   240   276

268   243

233 233 248 264   244

148   146

246   242   154

238   223   147   249   160   238

246   247   237   164

254   243 245   250   237

253   272

251   257   144   255   239

254   279   255   274

265   158   236

270   226   254   275

271   157   248   185   166   142

262 149 230   264   168 167   249

112 238 113   250 115 258   259   236   265

256   116   257 169 272   165

241   243

242 269   239 114   162 247   269   266

259   239 241   214   117 210   267

244   253   140   262   171   170   241

239 111   222   239   118

237   237   195   268   260

110   236 259   226   261   172   250 245   155

236 268 109   196 256   263

211 239   277   271   174 119   153

235   225   212   197   275 236 120 263

108   210   198   173 238 188 175 177   240

235   107   139 207 209   236 248 176   121

217   266   278   261   187 178   122

279   215   213   271   189 199   128

138   186   181   123

234 238 105 214 102   260   129   127 125

106   103 101 215 276 273   200 184   126 124 213

260   217 100 137   136   183   131

228 104   206 135 269 275   237

263   264   273   267 130 249

278   256   218   201 132 193

277   216 231   209 274

270 220 261   266   134 246 252

227 247   208   133   252

262 279   237 270 229   224   274

238   228   225 190   202 192

163   156   242   143   251

234 224 252 244   227 191   211 151

272 152 257   216 145   255 205 231

258   220

267   204 141   159   273   229

161   253   222

251 150 276   203

21

Answer on page 104

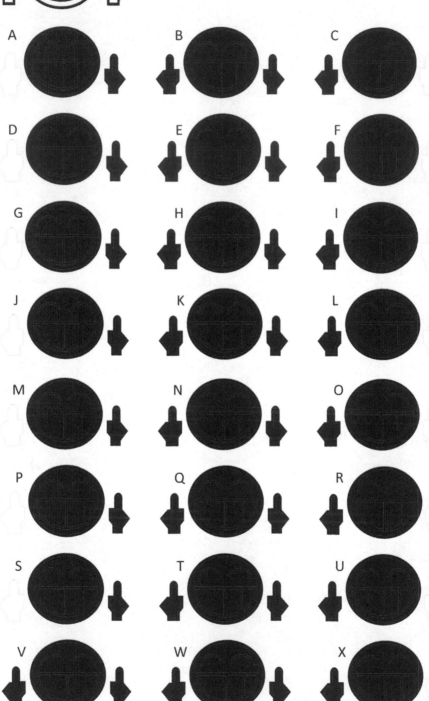

Some lazy-ass motherfucker really did a half-assed job on this drawing. Draw the other half of this shit.

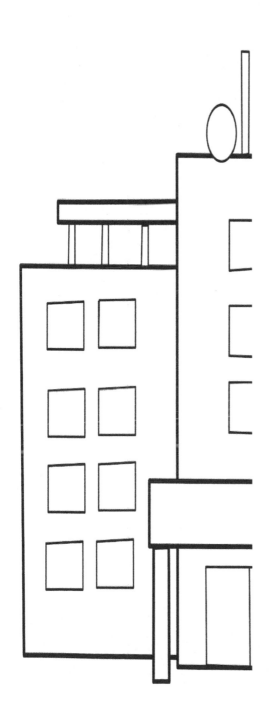

Which fucker doesn't belong?

Answer on page
104

24

Solve this bitch of a maze. Each finger is a separate maze to navigate, so it's really five fucking mazes in one. Ain't that a kick in the ass.

Answer on page
105

Math Squares

Answer on page 105

Try to fill in the missing numbers, bitch!

Use the numbers 1 to 9 to complete the equations and can be used more than once. Not good at math? You're fucked.

Each row is a math equation. Good luck with that shit. Work it in order of operations.

That's not all! Each column is a math equation, too. Surprise, bitch! Also order of operations.

8	x		-	4	**44**
/	■	+	■	/	
	-	6	x		**-11**
-	■	-	■	+	
7	+		x	9	**34**
1		**9**		**11**	

Figure out how the fuck you fit the numbered smaller boxes into the larger rectangle. You can't break up the shapes or change their orientation either, bitch, so don't even think of cheating that way!

Answer on page 105

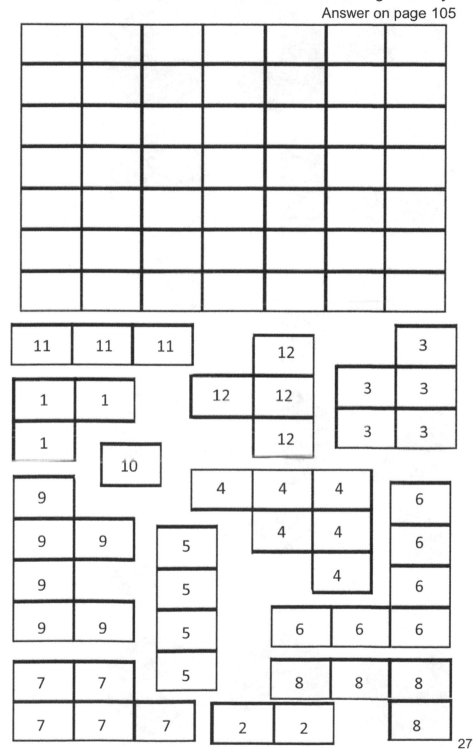

Here's your chance to be a motherfucking psychic! Predict the next shape in each fucking row. Answer on page 105

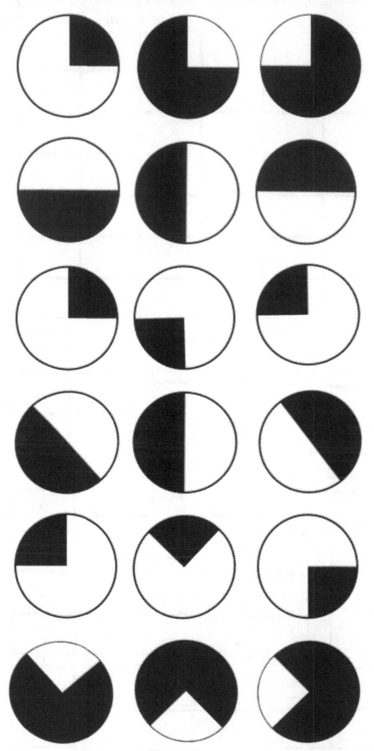

Letter Tiles

Answer on page 105

I can't understand this shit!

Move the fucking tiles around to make the correct phrase.

The three letters on each tile must stay together and in the given order, so don't try to cheat, motherfucker!

ET	POI	KE	AN '	I'D	P M
W B	ROM	I NG	SS .	HAT	SEE
OF	TH	R U	UT	D T	MY
L I	YO	FA	V I E	HEA	S F
UR	T G	TO	NT	I C	Y A

I'D					

One fucking cunt always has to be the difficult one. Find the asshole that's different from the rest.

Answer on page 105

Fallen Phrases

Answer on page 105

A fallen phrase is a fucked puzzle where all the letters have fallen to the bottom. They got jacked up on their way down, but remain in the same row. Complete this horse shit by filling the letters in the column they fall under. You start by filling in the one-letter columns, because those clearly don't have anywhere else to go in their column Don't make this shit harder than it has to be.

Also try filling in common one-, two- and three-letter words. I even gave your lucky ass an example.

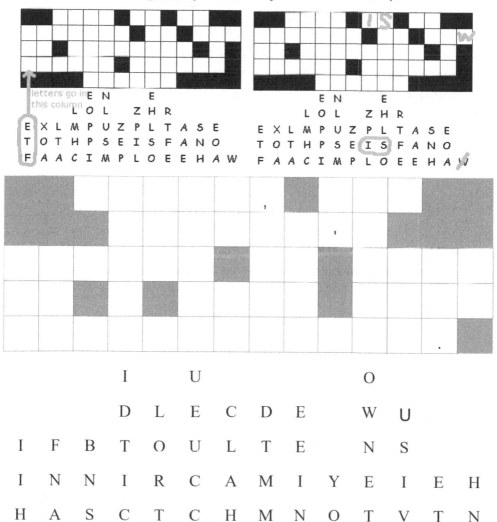

letters go in this column

E N   E
   L O L   Z H R
E X L M P U Z P L T A S E
T O T H P S E I S F A N O
F A A C I M P L O E E H A W

E N   E
   L O L   Z H R
E X L M P U Z P L T A S E
T O T H P S E I S F A N O
F A A C I M P L O E E H A W

      I   U   O
      D   L   E   C   D   E   W   U
I   F   B   T   O   U   L   T   N   S
I   N   N   I   R   C   A   M   I   Y   E   I   E   H
H   A   S   C   T   C   H   M   N   O   T   V   T   N

Ever play Sudoku? I bet your sorry ass hasn't!
These are the goddamn rules.

Answer on page 105

Numbers from 1 to 9 are inserted into sets that have 9 x 9 = 81 squares in whole. Every number can be used just once in every, 3x3 block, column and row, so don't reuse that shit.

- Every number can be used just once in the blocks of 3 x 3 = 9 square blocks. Use a number more than once, you fuck everything up.
- Each row of 9 numbers ought to contain all digits 1 through 9 in any order, so don't fucking miss any.
- Every column of 9 numbers should comprise all digits 1 through 9 in any order. Hope you can fucking count.

Here's a hint for your stupid ass: One way to figure out which numbers can go in each space is to use "process of elimination" by checking to see which other numbers are already included within each square – remember, no duplicates, asshole.

		5	9		6			8
	6				8		5	
	9			1		6		3
						3	9	7
			6		4			
7	5	8						
3		6		9			1	
	1		8				6	
5			2		1	7		

Can you find 14 of these  in the image?

Answer on page 106

Holy shit, that's a lot of circles! Someone should keep track of this shit. Count up all the circles.

Answer on page 106

I can't read any of these damn words. Unscramble this shit.

Answer on page 106

es,Y

I

nac,

Nwo

gte

het

uckf

out

fo

ym

y,aw

I

nur

no

neeci,aff

oshac,

dna

scus

drow.s

The damn goal consists of finding the black boxes in each grid.

The numbers given on the side and top of the grid indicate the numbers of consecutive black boxes in each line or column. Got that, bitches?

Here's a goddamn example: 3,3 on the left of a line indicates that there is, from left to right, a block of 3 black boxes then a block of 3 black boxes on this line. Have I lost your ass yet?
To solve the puzzle, you need to determine which cells will be black and which will be fucking empty. Determining which cells are to be left empty (called spaces) is as important as determining which to fill (called boxes). Later in the solving process, the spaces help determine where a clue (continuing block of boxes and a number in the legend) may spread. Solvers usually use a dot or a cross to mark cells they are certain are spaces.

It is also important never to fucking guess. Only cells that can be determined by damn logic should be filled. An example is shown here:

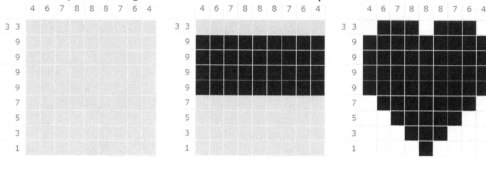

Answer on page 106

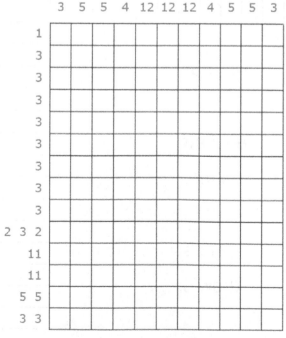

This shit's so plain. You should add some fucking color to this

FUCK this Fucking CRYPTOGRAM!

You are given a shit piece of text where each letter is substituted with a irrelevant damn number and you need to fucking decide which letters in the alphabet are being coded by the numbers you are given.

You need to use logic to crack this shit, so pull your head outta your ass and figure that crap out!

A	B	C	D	E	F	G	H	I

J	K	L	M	N	O	P	Q	R

S	T	U	V	W	X	Y	Z
			13				

Answer on page 106

```
__   __  __  __        __  __  __  __   ,   __  __  __
 1    8  17   4       21  12  14   1       15  26   4

     __  __  __  __  __  __      __  __
      1  23  25  25   6  14       8   7

__  __  __  __  __  __  __  __  __
12  11  12  24   6  12  16   6   4

                         W
__  __  __  __  __      __  __  __  __      __  __
20  23  18   1   4      13   8  18  21   1      24   1

    __  __  __  __  __  __  __  __  __  __  __  __
    24  10   1  23   7   7  24  20  24   4  10  15

    __  __      __  __  __  __      __  __
    15   8      17   4   4  15      17  14

        __  __  __  __  __  __  __ .
        21   4  17  12  10  21   1
```

38

Connect the damn dots from 100 to 202. All the other numbers are there just to fuck up your day!

Answer on page 106

218   258   230   278   240   276
       268   233 248 264   245 242 244 243
    233
103   223   104 109 110   246   113 114 121 122 249 132
102   101 106   105   271 243   245 247   131   135   133
238   246   270   262   253   250   136   134
       254   230   111   256   112   250   258 238
251   257   254   118   226   117 239   130   137
265   259   243   255   255   212 264 129
185   274   272   236   279   241   125 126   128 138
257   100 107   108 119   248   116 115   127   139
242   241   252   214   120 123   124   140
259   239   247   210 269   266
244   253   159 158   141   142 261   241   267
239   213   251   156   277 226   260
237   236   259   211   146   145   143   268
236   268   225   265   144   250 245   237
235   236   211 239   155   210   147   228 262   263   252
217   239   212   249   236   222   263   240
235   266   209   275 151 152   154   238   239
237   279   207   153   148   236 248   256   271
272   238   215   160 157 150   149   261   213   227 271 275
234   238   214   265   276   273   260   225 270 278
162   180 181   263   184 185 192 193 198   228   199
163   176   161 242   256 217   249 197   196 201 200
175   178   227   262   264   206   269   275
174   177   278 182   279 183   215   273 267 237
164   270   218   209
277   165   173 189   188 216 231   274 246
169 168   166   220   238   247   266   274
167   261   234   274   260   208   224 224
170   172   179 190   187 186 191 194   195 202   272
171   257   244   258   255   205   231 220   222
267   251   204 216   203   253   273   229   229

Now here's a shadow puppet they never let you make in school! Find the right fucking shadow.

Answer on page 106

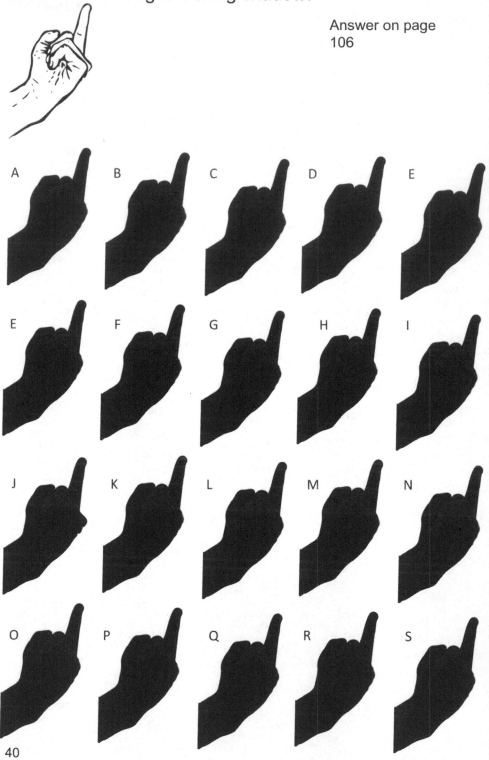

Start in the middle and find your way
the fuck out of this cock and balls!
(three mazes in one)

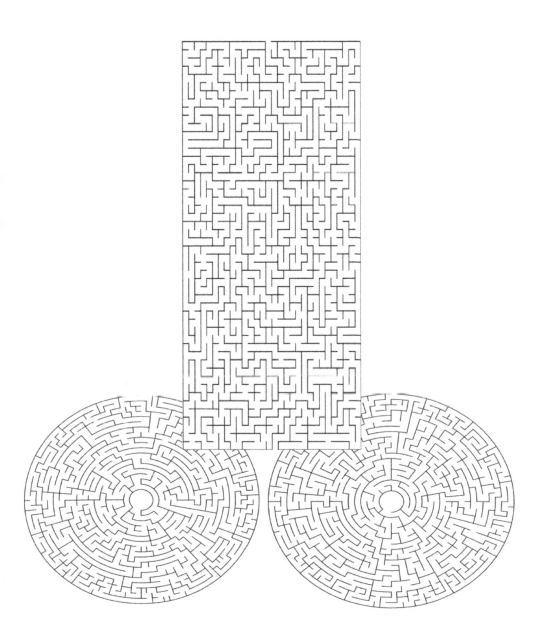

Figure out how the fuck you fit the numbered smaller shapes into the Larger honeycomb without changing the shapes or breaking them up!

Answer on page 107

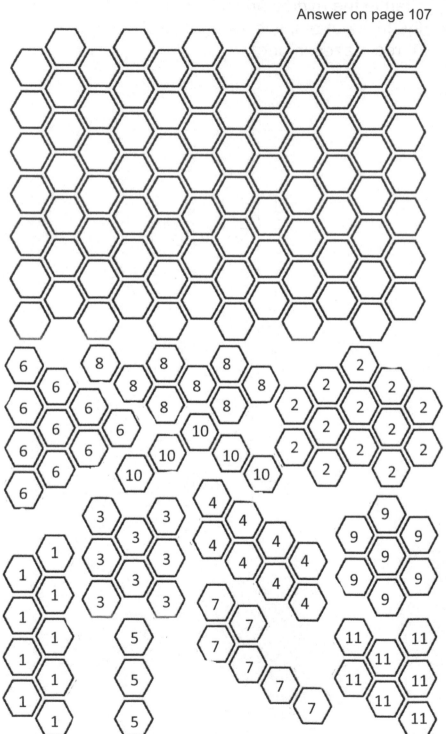

This picture's fucking fucked! Draw each image to it's correct square to fix the the motherfucker.

Image on page 107

A1 A2 A3 A4

B1 B2 B3 B4

C1 C2 C3 C4

D1 D2 D3 D4

	A	B	C	D
1				
2				
3				
4				

43

Number Blocks

Answer on page 107

Try to fill in the missing numbers if you can, bitch!

The missing numbers are from fucking 0 to 9.
The numbers in each row add up to the totals to the right.
The numbers in each column add up to the totals along the bottom. Numbers can be repeated, so do what you gotta do!
The diagonal lines also add up the totals to the right.
Good fucking luck! Complicated? Fuck yeah, it's complicated.

					39
2		3			28
	0		9	3	19
1		7	0	4	15
5	9		6		25
8		3		8	30
18	25	21	30	23	23

Think these pictures are the same? You're wrong, bitch!
Circle the 12 differences. Answer on page 107

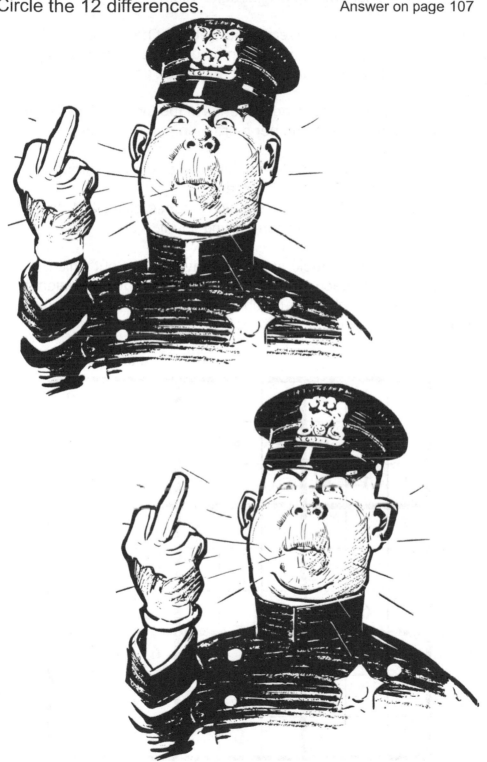

45

These are the goddamn fucking sudoku rules.

Numbers from 1 to 9 are inserted into sets that have 9 x 9 = 81 squares in whole. Every number can be used just once in every, 3x3 block, column and row, so don't reuse that shit.

- Every number can be used just once in the blocks of 3 x 3 = 9 square blocks. Use a number more than once, you fuck everything up.
- Each row of 9 numbers ought to contain all digits 1 through 9 in any order, so don't fucking miss any.
- Every column of 9 numbers should comprise all digits 1 through 9 in any order. Hope you can fucking count.

Here's a hint for your stupid ass: One way to figure out which numbers can go in each space is to use "process of elimination" by checking to see which other numbers are already included within each square – remember, no duplicates.

Answer on page 107

				1				9
		6	8	4				
4	1	2			6		8	
7					8	5	3	
2								8
	6	8	3					4
	8		9			6	4	2
				8	4	9		
9				5				

Which asshole does not belong?

Answer on page 108

47

Search for the shitty words in the list

Nutsack   Bastard   Fuckface

Assclown   Choad   Clusterfuck

Fuckstick   Asshole   Cockburger

Shitcunt   Rimjob   Peckerhead

Answer on page 108

```
                        N   L   T   Y
                        F   D   W   C
                M   J   N   H   X   Y
                J   D   O   R   Y   I
                H   A   B   V   C   F
                D   J   H   P   C   U
                C   K   H   F   S   C
                R   W   T   U   O   K
                H   L   J   G   P   F
                M   D   W   X   G   A
                V   E   W   S   Z   C
                P   X   I   O   S   E
                H   J   R   M   L   J
                V   D   E   Q   W   R
                P   J   G   S   X   V
                Y   J   R   X   S   R
                F   K   U   K   L   O
                U   W   B   C   E   T
            C   E   T   U   L   K   M   L   O       F   D   N   X
        C   M   L   O   G   F   D   C   V   N   J   L   M   E   I   Y   I
    O   P   L       Z   Q   R   J   N   V   X   O   M   A   S   S   H   O   L   E   F
X   B   N   M   L   J   H   F   I   S   R   Y   C   J   L   N   B   U   O   P   C   P
B   V   X   Q   W   R   V   H   J   M   V   C   F   H   C   O   P   G   P   F   S   V
Y   T   E   S   X   V   P   M   J   H   J   C   P   L   R   W   X   X   G   J   O   P
P   D   R   A   T   S   A   B   K   H   F   O   V   C   H   J   K   L   O   F   P   F
V   P   I   K   L   O   F   T   W   T   U   O   B   R   S   O   P   P   T   U   U   J
L   M   M   C   E   T   U   O   L   J   G   P   F   H   X   B   N   M   L   C   O   F
S   E   P   E   C   K   E   R   H   E   A   D   J   T   B   V   X   Q   K   R   T   U
Y   I   K   H   F   S   V   C   O   P   L   O   N   T   Y   T   E   S   X   V   O   G
F   T   W   T   U   O   P   R   W   X   P   U   U   O   P   F   T   X   S   R   J   L       R   Y
U   O   L   J   G   P   F   H   J   K   C   O   G   F   V   I   M   J   H   X   W   U   V   O   F
G   F   K   W   X   G   J   M   B   T   R   J   L   M   C   Y   I   K   H   K   O   S   M   P   N
L   M   C   W   S   Z   U   V   I   S   P   W   U   K   O   F   T   W   T   C   Y   M   N   W   D
U   V   A   I   O   S   W   H   L   M   N   O   S   M   P   U   B   E   I   P   C   O   O   U   T
G   J   S   P   U   S   S   D   N   L   T   Y   M   N   B   D   H   S   O   P   B   L   X   E   O
C   X   T   O   P   L   N   G   F   D   W   C   O   I   U   T   E   X   B   N   C   S   O   P   L
S   O   U   L   D   K   C   U   F   R   E   T   S   U   L   C   D   B   V   S   E   X   B   N
X   B   N   M   L   J   H   F   D   S   R   Y   I   J   B   C   O   Y   S   E   N   B   V
    V   X   Q   W   R   V   H   J   B   V   C   F   H   J   K   M   A   E   H   I   Y
        S   X   V   P   M   J   H   P   C   P   L   N   B   P   V   P   I   O
```

Find the dumbass that's trying to be different.

Answer on page 108

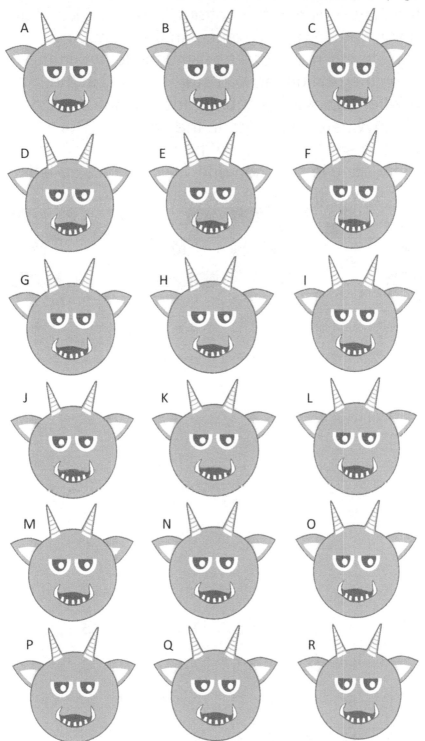

Fallen Phrases

Answer on page 108

A fallen phrase is a fucked puzzle where all the letters have fallen to the bottom. They got jacked up on their way down, but remain in the same row. Complete this horse shit by filling the letters in the column they fall under. You start by filling in the one-letter columns, because those clearly don't have anywhere else to go in their column. Don't make this shit harder than it has to be.

Also try filling in common one-, two- and three-letter words. I even gave your lucky ass an example.

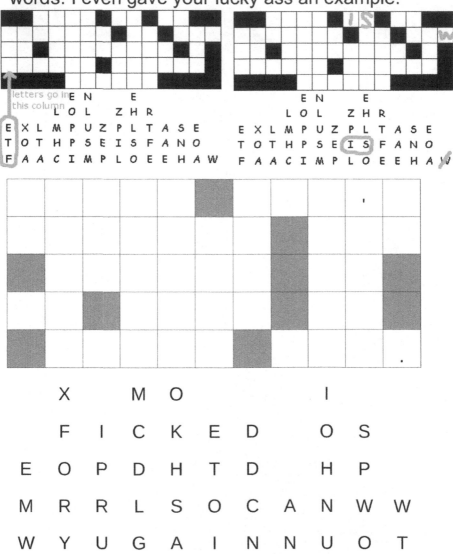

letters go in this column

```
      E  N        E                    E  N        E
      L  O  L     Z  H  R            L  O  L     Z  H  R
E  X  L  M  P  U  Z  P  L  T  A  S  E    E  X  L  M  P  U  Z  P  L  T  A  S  E
T  O  T  H  P  S  E  I  S  F  A  N  O    T  O  T  H  P  S  E  I  S  F  A  N  O
F  A  A  C  I  M  P  L  O  E  E  H  A  W F  A  A  C  I  M  P  L  O  E  E  H  A  W
```

```
     X        M  O                    I
     F     I  C  K  E  D           O  S
  E  O  P  D  H  T  D           H  P
  M  R  R  L  S  O  C  A  N  W  W
  W  Y  U  G  A  I  N  N  U  O  T
```

50

Math Squares

Answer on page 108

Try to fill in the missing numbers, bitch!

Use the numbers 1 to 9 to complete the equations and can be used more than once. Not good at math? You're fucked.

Each row is a math equation. Good luck with that shit. Work it in order of operations.

That's not all! Each column is a math equation, too. Surprise, bitch! Also order of operations.

	x	3	-		**20**
/	■	+	■	-	
3	-		x	12	**-45**
-	■	/	■	+	
	+	2	x		**26**
-5		**5**		**4**	

Can you find 13 of these  in the image? My
fucking eyes are bleeding just looking at this

Answer on page 108

Ever play Sudoku? I bet you fucking haven't! These are the wanked rules.

Numbers from 1 to 9 are inserted into sets that have 9 x 9 = 81 squares in whole. Every number can be used just once in every, 3x3 block, column and row, so don't reuse the goddamn shit.

- Every number can be used just once in the blocks of 3 x 3 = 9 square blocks. Use a number more than once, your fucked.
- Each row of 9 numbers must fucking contain all digits 1 through 9 in any order, so don't fucking miss that shit.
- Every column of 9 numbers should comprise all digits 1 through 9 in any order. Hope you can fucking count, bitch.

Here's a hint for your stupid ass: One way to figure out which numbers can go in each space is to use "process of elimination" by checking to see which other numbers are already included within each square – remember, no duplicates.

				4	6			
	7			8		3	4	5
		4				9	7	
2		9	1					4
			2		3			
1					8	5		3
	1	2				7		
7	5	3		2			1	
			5	7				

Letter Tiles

Answer on page 109

What the fuck is this shit?!

Move the piece of shit tiles around to make the correct phrase.

The three letters on each tile must stay together and in the given order, so don't try to cheat, motherfucker!

I T	R S	T A T	P H A	H A T	A B
S O	O W L	O U T	A N D	B E T	E M E
A L	.	S H	R T E	T H A	U P
D E	A T	O U L	N T	O F	I C
S M A	A N	N T			

I C					

What comes next in each line, bitch?

Answer on page 109

Connect the dots from 100 to 124
Don't let the extra numbers fool you!

Answer on page 109

230
218   258   268   278   240   276
                                                                    243
        165   233   233 248 264   245   244
                            246   253   249   132
238   246   223   250   242   238
                254   243   245   114   237
                                        113   237
        257   255   115   272   129
251   254   159   255   274   130   239
        265   279   254   275   236
271   270   226   248   185   166   133
            230   168   167   249
262   264   258   236   265
        238   269   250   259   257 169   272
256   241   212   135
        242   239
259   239   241   214   128   247 243   269 266
244   253   262   171   210   267
        239   110 111   170   241
            107 108   109   112 195   239   268   260
237
        105 106 259   226   261   172   250   245   263   136
236   104   225   237   196   256   271   118
235   103   127   212   211 239   277 197   236 174 117   263   119
                            210   198   275   120
235   217   266   207   209   173   238 188 175 240
        279   278   116   236 248 176   177
102   215   213   271   189   261 121   187 178   179
        126   214   199   186   181
            234   238   247   276   273   260   180
260   228   265   184 183 182
        101   217   206   215   122   275 194   213
263   277   278   256   218   273   267 237 249
        220   261   216 231   209   201   193
270   100   227   123   266   274 246 252
        124   279   270   229   208   224   274 252
142   262   238   237 228   225 190   202 192   251
    234   224   252   244   242   141
                                    227   191   211
        272   125   257   216   137   255 205   231   143
        267   258   220
            131   204   138   134   273   229
                                140   222
            251   139   276   253   144   203

56

Help this fucker find his shadow.

Answer on page 109

A
B
C
D
E

F
G
H
I
J

K
L
M
N
O

P
Q
R
S
T

That is a fuckload of circles! How many circles are in a fuckload? Count them and find out.

Answer on page 109

The fucked rules of a cryptogram puzzle:

Answer on page 109

You are given a shit piece of text where each letter is substituted with a irrelevant damn number and you need to fucking decide which letter in the native alphabet is being coded by the numbers you are given.

You need to use logic and knowledge of the letters and words of our goddamn language to crack this shit.

A	B	C	D	E	F	G	H	I
							18	

J	K	L	M	N	O	P	Q	R

S	T	U	V	W	X	Y	Z

```
 __  __      __  __  __      __  __  __   '  __
 2   24      25  3   19      17  3   23      1

 __  __  __  __      __  __  '      __  __  __  __
 16  2   14  26      6   26         1   10  14  26

 __      __  __  __  '      __  __  __      __
 10      6   10  8          12  26  1       10

 __  __  __  '      __  __  __  __  __      __  __
 4   10  22         17  22  2   21  26      1   3

 h   __  __  __  ,      h   __  __  __      __
 18  26  16  16         18  10  21  26      10

     __  __  __  __      __  __  __  __   .
     23  2   4   26      1   22  2   8
```

Who fucked these words up? Goddammit, now you have your work cut out for you. Unscramble each of the words to make a phrase that makes sense.

Answer on page 109

eHy

tuao

orcect,r

uiqt

pmneitagr

hwti

ym

ceusr

,dosrw

uoy

mhorte

irklof.ft

This pictures fucking jacked! Draw the rest.

The damn goal consists of finding the black boxes in each grid.

The numbers given on the side and top of the grid indicate the numbers of consecutive black boxes in each line or column. Got that, bitches?

Here's a goddamn example: 3,3 on the left of a line indicates that there is, from left to right, a block of 3 black boxes then a block of 3 black boxes on this line. Have I lost your ass yet?

To solve a puzzle, one needs to determine which cells will be black and which will be fucking empty. Determining which cells are to be left empty (called spaces) is as important as determining which to fill (called boxes). Later in the solving process, the spaces help determine where a clue (continuing block of boxes and a number in the legend) may spread. Solvers usually use a dot or a cross to mark cells they are certain are spaces.

It is also important never to fucking guess. Only cells that can be determined by damn logic should be filled. An example is shown here:

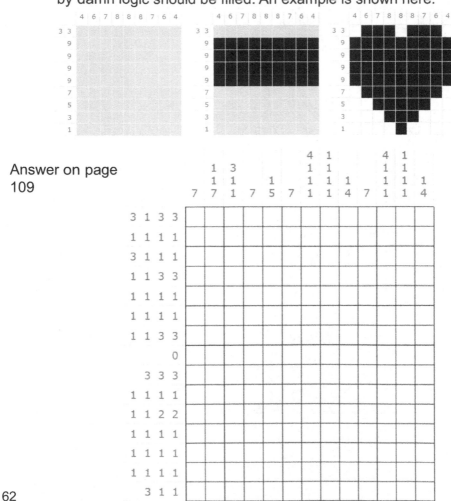

Answer on page 109

This image has a lot of fucking snakes. See if you can find 13 of those fuckers

Answer on page 110

Color this shit, and stay in the fucking lines! You're not a goddamn toddler.

Fucking Sudoku! Follow these goddamn rules.

110 Answer on page

Numbers from 1 to 9 are inserted into sets that have 9 x 9 = 81 squares in whole. Every number can be used just once in every, 3x3 block, column and row, so don't reuse that shit.

- Every number can be used just once in the blocks of 3 x 3 = 9 square blocks. Use a number more than once, you fuck everything up.
- Each row of 9 numbers ought to contain all digits 1 through 9 in any order, so don't fucking miss any.
- Every column of 9 numbers should comprise all digits 1 through 9 in any order. Hope you can fucking count.

Here's a hint for your stupid ass: One way to figure out which numbers can go in each space is to use "process of elimination" by checking to see which other numbers are already included within each square – remember, no duplicates or you're fucked.

				1		2	6	5
					6		4	3
			2			8		
	8		5	6		9		4
	4						5	
5		9		4	8		2	
		1			3			
8	7		1					
4	9	6		5				

Figure out how the fuck you fit the numbered smaller boxes into the larger rectangle. You can't break up the shapes or change their orientation either, bitch, so don't even think of cheating that way!

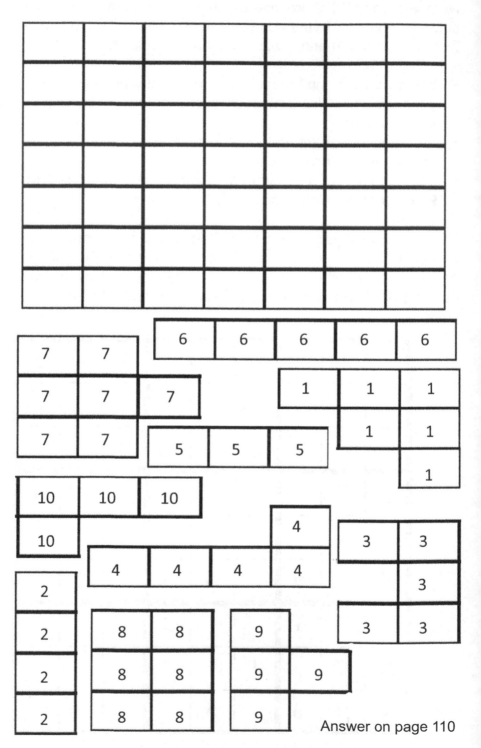

Answer on page 110

These pictures are not the same, fuck!
Circle the 10 differences.

Answer on page 110

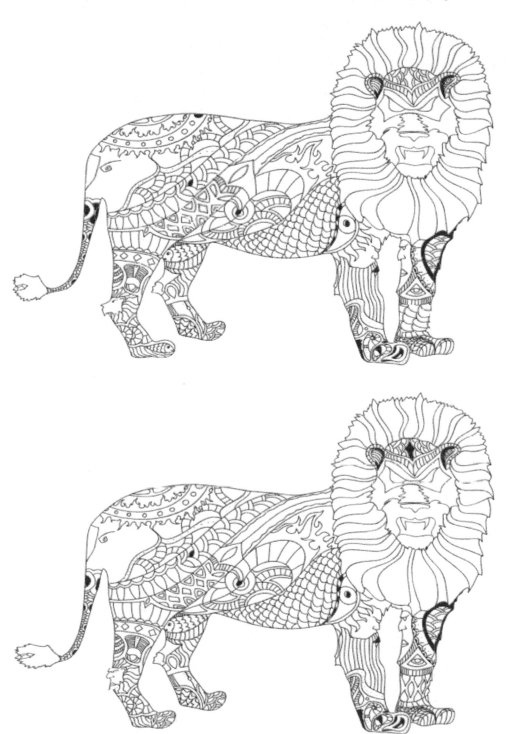

Here's a list of words to expand your vocabulary.
See if you can pull them out of this shitpile of letters

Bumhole	Shite	Cuntflaps
Wankface	Scrote	Shithouse
Pissartist	Cock	Knobcheese
Jizzbreath	Fuckwit	Arsebastard

```
                    N  L  T  Y
                    F  D  W  C
              M  J  N  V  X  Y
              S  D  S  R  Y  I
              H  C  B  V  C  F          Answer on page 110
              L  J  R  P  C  P
              C  K  H  O  S  V
              R  W  T  U  T  P
              H  B  J  G  P  E
              M  U  W  X  G  J
              V  M  W  S  Z  U
              P  H  I  O  S  W
              H  O  N  M  L  J
              V  L  S  Q  W  C
              P  E  B  S  U  V
              Y  J  H  N  S  R
              F  K  T  K  L  O
              U  F  T  C  E  T
          C  E  T     L  L  J  M  L  O        F  D  N  X
          C  M  L  O  A  F  D  W  V  N  J  L  M  E  I  Y  I
    O  P  L     Z  Q  G  P  N  V  X  Y  M  H  J  S  H  I  T  E  F
 X  B  N  M  L  J  H  S  D  S  R  Y  I  J  L  N  B  U  O  P  C  P
 B  V  X  Q  W  R  V  H  J  B  V  C  F  H  C  O  P  G  P  F  S  V
 Y  E  C  A  F  K  N  A  W  H  P  C  P  L  R  W  X  X  G  J  O  P
 P  F  H  X  S  R  Y  I  K  H  F  S  V  D  H  J  K  L  O  F  K  F
 V  P  I  K  L  O  F  T  W  T  U  O  P  R  R  O  P  P  T  U  C  J
 L  M  M  C  E  T  U  O  L  J  G  P  F  H  X  A  N  M  L  J  O  F
 S  E  C  M  L  O  G  F  D  W  X  G  J  M  B  V  T  Q  W  R  C  U
 Y  H  K  H  K  N  O  B  C  H  E  E  S  E  Y  T  E  S  X  V  O  G
 F  T  W  T  U  O  P  R  W  X  P  T  U  O  P  F  H  X  A  R  J  L        R  Y
 U  A  L  J  G  P  F  H  J  K  E  O  G  F  V  P  M  J  H  B  W  U  V  O  F
 G  E  D  W  X  G  J  M  B  F  R  J  L  M  I  Y  I  F  H  K  E  S  M  P  U
 L  R  E  W  S  Z  S  H  I  T  H  O  U  S  E  F  T  U  T  C  Y  S  N  B  D
 U  B  X  I  O  S  W  P  L  M  N  O  S  M  P  U  B  C  I  P  C  O  R  U  T
 G  Z  O  P  U  R  E  D  N  L  T  A  M  N  B  D  H  K  O  P  B  C  X  A  O
 C  Z  E  O  P  L  N  G  F  D  R  C  O  I  U  T  E  W  B  N  E  S  O  P  L
 S  I  P  L  D  Z  Q  G  J  T  V  X  Y  M  P  G  D  I  V  X  E  X  B  N
 X  J  N  M  L  J  H  F  I  S  R  Y  I  J  B  C  O  T  T  E  N  B  V
    V  X  Q  W  R  V  S  J  B  V  C  F  H  J  K  M  P  F  H  I  Y
       S  X  V  T  M  J  H  P  C  P  L  N  B  P  V  P  I  O
```

Number Blocks

Answer on page 111

Try to fill in the missing numbers if you can, asshole!

The missing numbers are integers (that means it's a whole number, goddammit) from 0 to 9.
The numbers in each row add up to the totals to the right.
The numbers in each column add up to the totals along the bottom. Numbers can be repeated, so don't get fucked and don't be an ass!
The diagonal lines also add up the totals to the right.
Good fucking luck!

						36
	2		9	4	0	28
3	1	9		4		27
4		6	8	2	7	32
2	4		2			22
1		5		5	6	34
8	5		0			28
25	25	37	30	24	30	30

Find the one fucking image that is different from the rest.

Answer on page 111

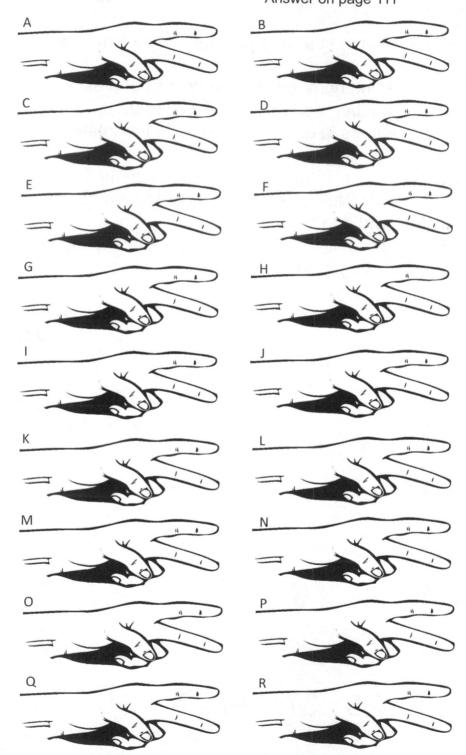

70

Answer on page 111

Solve this bitch of a maze. Each finger is a separate maze to navigate, so it's really four fucking mazes in one. More fun than a bag of dicks!

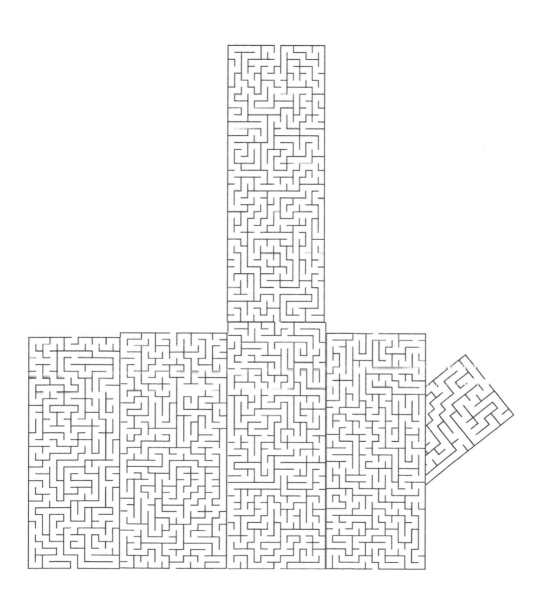

Letter Tiles

Answer on page 111

Fuck is this messed up shit?!

Move the damn tiles around to
make the correct phrase.

The three letters on each tile must
stay together and in the given order,
so don't try to cheat, dammit!

TH	YBO	IT	FUC	SN '	DOE
DEA	DY.	K–F	FU	FU	T'S
FU	T H	TY,	WHA	E B	CK,
!	CK–	URT	L?	CKI	AN
IG	UCK				

WHA					

Numbers from 1 to 9 are inserted into sets that have 9 x 9 = 81 squares in whole. Every number can be used just once in every, 3x3 block, column and row, so don't reuse that shit.

- Every number can be used just once in the blocks of 3 x 3 = 9 square blocks. Use a number more than once, you fuck everything up.
- Each row of 9 numbers ought to contain all digits 1 through 9 in any order, so don't fucking miss any.
- Every column of 9 numbers should comprise all digits 1 through 9 in any order. Hope you can fucking count.

Here's a hint for your stupid ass: One way to figure out which numbers can go in each space is to use "process of elimination" by checking to see which other numbers are already included within each square – remember, no duplicates.

7					6			
	9	1		5	8	4		
4	8							2
8				7		2		
	2		9		3		7	
		5		4				3
5							8	1
		8	5	1		3	4	
			8					5

Search for the jacked up words

Answer on page 111

Wingnut   Asshat   Jizzmuffin

Fuckwit   Prick   Buttmunch

Bitchtit   Shittiest   Shitspitter

Dickbag   Shitlicker   Dumbfuck

Dickweed   Lameass

```
                    E  D  N  L  T  Y  M
                    N  P  R  I  C  K  O
              Z  Q  G  J  N  V  X  W  M
              J  H  F  D  S  R  I  I  J
              R  V  H  J  B  N  C  F  H
              V  P  M  J  G  P  C  P  L
              R  Y  I  N  H  F  S  V  C
              O  F  U  W  T  U  O  P  R
              T  T  O  L  J  G  P  F  H
              O  G  F  D  W  S  G  J  M
              J  L  M  E  W  S  Z  U  V
              W  U  V  X  I  A  S  W  P
              Z  Q  G  J  N  E  L  H  H
              J  H  F  D  S  M  W  C  V
              R  V  H  J  B  A  X  N  P
              V  P  M  J  H  L  S  U  Y
              G  Y  I  K  H  K  L  M  F
              O  A  S  S  H  A  T  T  U
              T  U  B  L  J  M  L  T  G
              O  G  F  K  W  V  N  U  L
              J  N  V  X  C  M  H  B  K
              D  S  R  Y  I  I  L  N  B
              J  B  V  C  F  H  D  O  P
        E  S  X  V     J  H  P  C  P  L  R  W  X        J  O  P  R
     F  H  X  S  R  Y     K  H  T  I  W  K  C  U  F     O  F  P  F  H  X
  R  P  I  K  L  O  F  T  W  T  U  O  P  R  S  O  P  P  T  U  G  J  M  B  R
T  L  M  M  C  E  T  U  O  L  J  G  P  F  H  X  B  N  M  L  J  O  F  T  Y  T  G
V  S  H  I  T  S  P  I  T  T  E  R  G  J  M  B  V  X  Q  W  R  T  U  O  P  N  P
P  Y  I  R  H  F  S  V  C  O  P  L  O  F  T  Y  T  E  S  X  V  O  G  F  V  N  G
Y  F  T  W  E  D  O  P  R  W  X  P  T  R  E  K  C  I  L  T  I  H  S  M  I  Y  Z
F  U  O  L  J  K  U  F  H  J  K  E  O  G  F  V  P  M  J  H  X  W  U  F  O  F  S
U  G  F  D  D  X  C  M  M  B  F  R  J  L  M  R  Y  I  K  H  K  O  F  M  P  U  L
G  L  M  E  E  S  Z  I  B  W  S  P  W  U  V  O  F  T  W  T  C  U  M  N  B  D  W
L  U  V  X  E  O  S  W  L  F  M  N  O  S  M  P  U  B  E  I  M  C  O  I  U  T  X
U  G  J  O  W  U  R  E  D  T  U  T  Y  M  N  B  D  H  S  Z  P  B  C  X  E  O  S
Q  C  X  E  K  P  L  N  G  F  C  C  G  O  I  U  T  E  Z  B  N  E  S  O  P  L  L
E  S  O  P  C  D  Z  Q  G  J  N  H  K  Y  M  P  G  I  T  I  T  H  C  T  I  B  E
   X  S  H  I  T  T  I  E  S  T  R  S  I  J  B  J  O  Y  T  E  N  B  V  X  Q
   B  V  X  D  W  R  V  H                    P  F  H  I  Y  T  E  E
   T  E  S  X  V  P                          P  I  O  P  F  H
```

Math Squares

Answer on page 111

Try to fill in the missing numbers!

Use the numbers 1 to 9 to complete the equations and can be used more than once. Not good at math? You're fucked.

Each row is a math equation. Good luck with that shit. Work it in order of operations.

That's not all! Each column is a math equation, too. Surprise, bitch! Also order of operations.

	x	3	+		-	20	3
+	■	x	■	+	■	/	
8	+		/	2	-		1
/	■	/	■	x	■	-	
	x	1	+		/	3	5
x	■	-	■	/	■	+	
6	+		+	18	x		51

29	9	9	1

Connect the dots from 100 to 129

Answer on page 112

Don't let the extra numbers fuck with you!

143　　230　　144
258
218　　101　　102　　278　　240　　276
141　　233　　233　　248　　264　　245　　244　　162　　243
223　　268　　246　　242　　153
238　　246　　103　　249　　145　　164　　238
254　　152　　243　245　　247　　250　　237　　237
257　　253　　272　　159
251　　255　　274　　157　　239
254　　279　　255
265　　104　　236
270　　100　105　　254　　275
271　　248　　185　　166　　142
160　　230　　226　　155　　168　　167　　249
262　　264　　147　　236　　163
238　　146　　258　　265
256　　250　　259　　257　　169　　272
241　　107　　212　　243　　156
242　　269　　239　　266
241　　214　　261　　247　　269
259　　239　　130　　210　　267
244　　171　　170　　241
253　　222　　262
239　　239　　260
135　　110　　195
237　　237　　226　　268
236　　259　　172　　250　　245　　154
236　　106　　111　　109　108　256　　271　　263
268　　225　　277　　174　　150
235　　211　　239　　197
131　　212　　196　　236　　263
217　　210　　209　　198　　275　　188　　175　　240
235　　266　　132　　207　　173　　238　　177
113　　278　　115　　236　　248　176
148　　279　　215　　213　　261
120　　118　　199　　187　　178
151　　136　　214　　189　　186　　181　　179
238　　271　　276　　273　　260　　180
234　　265　　114　　184　　183　　182
228　　200
260　　217　　158　　264　　119　　269　　275　　194　　213
263　　149
278　　256　　112　121　218　117　116　267　　237　　249　　273
277　　216　　231　　193
270　　220　　261　　209　　201
227　　247　　266　　274　　246　　252
279　　208
262　　237　　270　229　　224　　274　　252
161　　137　　238　　228　　123　　190　　125　202　192
234　　224　252　　244　　242　　227　　251
225　　128　　191　　215
272　　134　　255　　205　　211
257　　216　　231　　165
138　　258　　220
267　　124　　229
133　　204　　139　　253　　222
273
251　　140　　276　　122129　　127126　　203

If you can't find the shadow that matches, go fuck yourself!

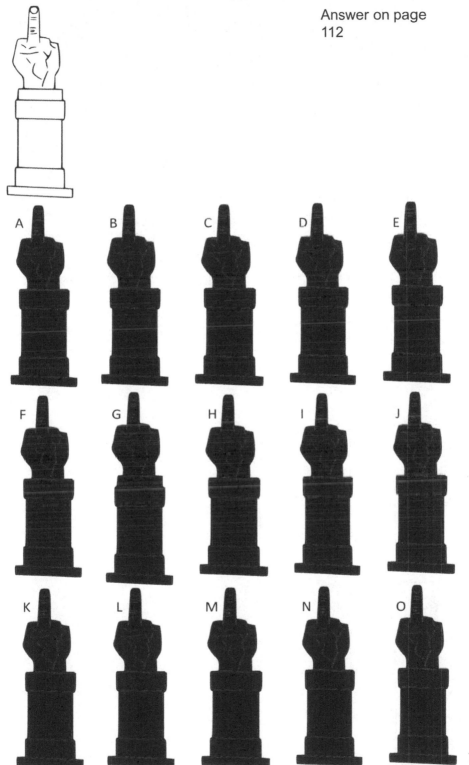

Answer on page 112

This picture's fucked! Draw each image to its corresponding square to fix this shit or we are all fucked.

Answer on page 112

A1

A2

A3

B1

B2

B3

B4

C1

C2

C3

C4

	A	B	C	D
1				
2				
3				
4	Leave This Square Blank			

D1

D2

D3

D4

Fallen Phrases

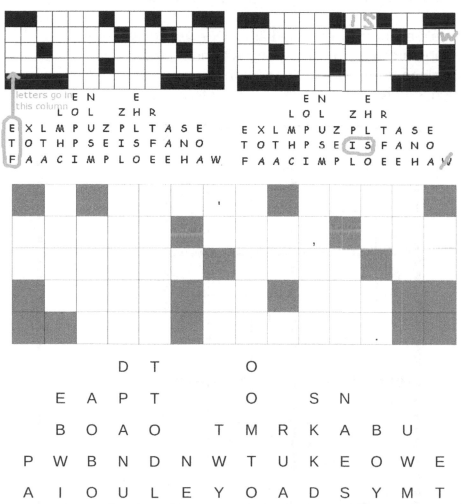

Answer on page 112

A fallen phrase is a fucked puzzle where all the letters have fallen to the bottom. They got jacked up on their way down, but remain in the same row. Complete this horse shit by filling the letters in the column they fall under. You start by filling in the one-letter columns, because those clearly don't have anywhere else to go in their column. Don't make this shit harder than it has to be.

Also try filling in common one-, two- and three-letter words. I even gave your lucky ass an example.

letters go in this column

E N   E
   L O L   Z H R
E X L M P U Z P L T A S E
T O T H P S E I S F A N O
F A A C I M P L O E E H A W

E N   E
   L O L   Z H R
E X L M P U Z P L T A S E
T O T H P S E I S F A N O
F A A C I M P L O E E H A W

D T   O

E A P T   O   S N

B O A O   T M R K A B U

P W B N D N W T U K E O W E

A I O U L E Y O A D S Y M T

79

Ever play Sudoku? I bet your sorry ass hasn't!
These are the goddamn rules.

Answer on page 112

Numbers from 1 to 9 are inserted into sets that have 9 x 9 = 81 squares in whole. Every number can be used just once in every, 3x3 block, column and row, so don't reuse that shit.

- Every number can be used just once in the blocks of 3 x 3 = 9 square blocks. Use a number more than once, you fuck everything up.
- Each row of 9 numbers ought to contain all digits 1 through 9 in any order, so don't fucking miss any.
- Every column of 9 numbers should comprise all digits 1 through 9 in any order. Hope you can fucking count.

Here's a hint for your stupid ass: One way to figure out which numbers can go in each space is to use "process of elimination" by checking to see which other numbers are already included within each square – remember, no duplicates.

7					6			
	9	1		5	8	4		
4	8							2
8				7		2		
	2		9		3		7	
		5		4				3
5							8	1
		8	5	1		3	4	
			8					5

Figure out this cryptogram shit:

Answer on page 112

You are given a shit piece of text where each letter is substituted with a irrelevant damn number and you Need to fucking decide which letter in the native alphabet is being coded by the numbers you are given.

You need to use logic and knowledge of the letters and words of our goddamn language to crack this shit.

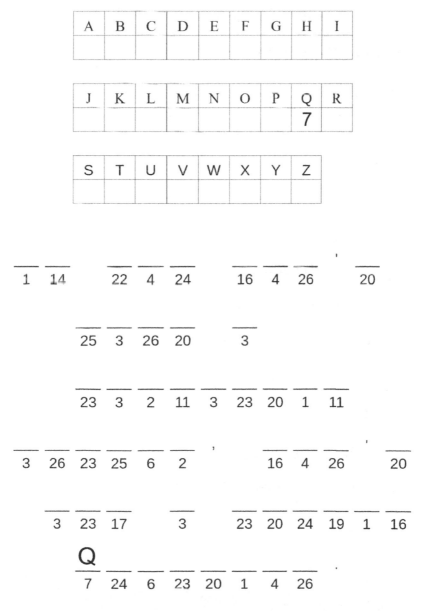

A	B	C	D	E	F	G	H	I

J	K	L	M	N	O	P	Q	R
							7	

S	T	U	V	W	X	Y	Z

1 14   22 4 24   16 4 26 ' 20

25 3 26 20   3

23 3 2 11 3 23 20 1 11

3 26 23 25 6 2 ,   16 4 26 ' 20

3 23 17   3   23 20 24 19 1 16

Q 7 24 6 23 20 1 4 26 .

Oh shit, the scramble got even more complicated!
Unscramble the motherfucking letters in each phrase.

Answer on page 112

r' sacs uYek s onthuac

tcck iFhs esuhil

mit vcoBnie itGehgs

ehiechi Bet dosg sntt

efmc !uk

Hlydll oBoe

k!ph UcSiF tu

sayk lb lScum

Hlhs allitboys

i ukomfr ceA-ntct

uksw cd FSmyieea

-i!rethofctuks-hM

ht siGr oo e paup

catc tfk aehulWh !atu

slokBoi tiuuh cn gfcndF

Circle the 13 fucking differences. Can you find them all, bitch?

Answer on page 112

83

Which dumbass does not belong?

Answer on page 113

Number Blocks

Answer on page 113

Try to fill in the missing numbers if you can, asshole!

The missing numbers are integers (that means it's a damn whole number) from 0 to 9.
The numbers in each row add up to the totals to the right.
The numbers in each column add up to the totals along the bottom. Numbers can be repeated, so don't get fucked and don't be an ass!
The diagonal lines also add up the totals to the right.
Good fucking luck!

						38
1		5	3		6	20
3	7	2		5		24
	8	0	8	7	3	30
2	5		4		8	37
		1		0	4	18
8	6		9		9	37
24	31	19	36	26	30	21

85

Letter Tiles

I can't fucking read this shit!

Move the goddamn tiles around to make the correct phrase.

The three letters on each tile must stay together and in the given order, so don't try to cheat, asswipe!

CT,	OP	S Y	DEA	OF	PIE
REC	CO	G M WEA	T .		UTO
TIN	SHU	ST	COR	CE	ORD
RRE	R	WR	A OU	Y S	

DEA				

What a kickass dragon! Have fucking fun coloring this sexy-ass bitch!

There are a lot of assholes in the world. This page alone has a shit-ton of them! Count 'em up

Answer on page 113

You took too long finding the fucker that's different, and now they're all dead. Fucking hell! Well, see if you can find the different one anyway.

Answer on page 113

I don't know what the fuck this is, but only half of it's there. Draw the other half of that shit.

What comes next in the line, fucker? Answer on page 113

91

Connect the dots from 100 to 117
Don't get screwed by extra numbers.

Answer on page 113

230

218   258   278   240   159   276

268   243

147   233   233   248   264   244

143   245   151   156

223   146   246   242

238   246   249   152   153   238

145   243   245   247   237   237

254   250

257   144   255   253   272   142

251   239

254   279   255   274   148

265   255   140   236

270   163   226   254   275   150

271   185   166

141   248   162   168   167   249

262   134   230   139   236   160

238   138   250   258   265

256   241   259   169   272

242   269   239   212   257   243   165

259   239   241   109   214   247   269   266

108   110   210   267

244   253   161   262   171   170   241

239   222   195   239   135   260

136   237   268

237   236   259   226   261   172   250   245   149

236   268   225   196   256   263

235   211   239   277   271   174   137   155

131   212   124   197   275   236   263

217   198   173   238   188   175   240

235   266   128   207   209   236   248   176   177

129   279   215   213   271   278   261   178

130   127   214   132   189   199   187   179

238   276   273   260   186   181   180

234   228   265   133   184   183   182

260   119   120   217   206   200   269   275   194   213

263   121   278   256   264   229   218   215   273   267   237   249   164

277   216   231   209   201   193

270   220   261   227   247   266   274   246   252

262   279   237   270   208   224   274   252

106   238   112   202   192

154   105   107   111   190   113   251

234   224   252   244   118   225   126

123   227   191   211

272   104   257   122   216   100   117   255   205   231   228

116   220

267   125   204   101   114   229

157   103   251   102   276   242   115   273   158   203   222

Search for the damn up words!

Answer on page 113

Knobhead   Twat   Shitbag

Pissflaps   Damn   Cocknose

Bitchtits   Prick   Dickweed

Shitpouch   Wanker   Arsebadger

Bollocks   Jizzcock   Fuckbucket

```
                              N B D
                            O I K T E
                            Y M N G D
                            I J O C O
                            F H B K M
                            P L H B K
                            V C E P C
                            P R A X O
                            F H D K C
                            J M D F Z
                            U V W S Z
                            W D L M I
                            J H A D J
                            R V H M H
                            V P M J N
                            R Y I K B
                            O F T W E
                  T W O T   T U A L E
              M C E P   O L J M   O R F D N
  P U R S     C M L O R F D W V N S L M E I
  S O P T     Z Q G J N I X Y M E J K F S V
  X B W M L J H F D S R Y I B L N B U O P
  B A X Q W A N K D R V C A H C O P G P F
  T T E S X V P M J H P D P L R W X X G J
  P F D X S R Y I K H G S V C H J K L O F
  V P I E L O F T W E U O P R S O P P T U
  L M M C E T U O R J G P F H X B N M L J       B V T J
  S T C M L W G F D E H C U O P T I H S R     T Y T D U
  Y E K H F S K C O P L O F T Y T E S X V U O P F U W
  F K W T U O P C W X P C U O P F H B O L L O C K S J
  U C L J S P F H I K E K G F V P M J H X C O I P D R
  G U D W T G J M B D R N L M R Y I K H K B C A P O V
  L B E W I Z U V W S P O U V O F T W T C E L A P L
  U K X I T S W P L M N S S M P U B E I P F L O N
  G C O P H R E D N L K E M N B D H S O S N B V
  C U E O C L N G F D W C O I U T E X S N I Y
  S F P L T Z Q G J N V X I M P G D I V X
  X B S H I T B A G S R Y I R B C P Y T
    V X Q B R V H J B V C F H P K M P
      E S X V P M J H P C P L N B
```

Fallen Phrases

Answer on page 114

A fallen phrase is a fucked puzzle where all the letters have fallen to the bottom. They got jacked up on their way down, but remain in the same row. Complete this horse shit by filling the letters in the column they fall under. You start by filling in the one-letter columns, because those clearly don't have anywhere else to go in their column.

Don't make this shit harder than it has to be.

Also try filling in common one-, two- and three-letter words. I even gave your lucky ass an example.

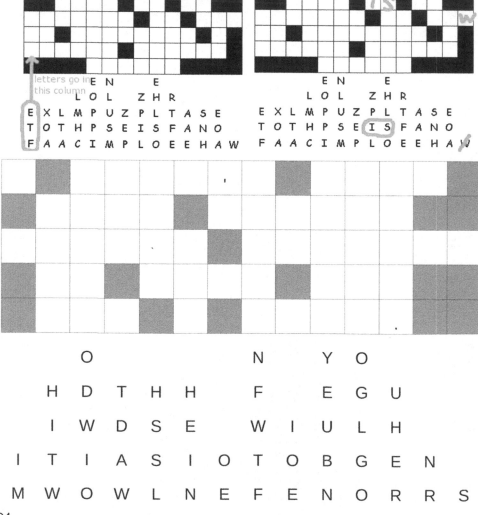

letters go in this column

```
  E  N        E
    L O L    Z H R
E X L M P U Z P L T A S E
T O T H P S E I S F A N O
F A A C I M P L O E E H A W
```

```
            I S
                      W
  E  N        E
    L O L    Z H R
E X L M P U Z P L T A S E
T O T H P S E I S F A N O
F A A C I M P L O E E H A W
```

```
    O           N       Y   O
  H D T H H     F     E   G   U
  I W D S E     W   I   U   L   H
I   T I A S I O T O B G E N
M W O W L N E F E N O R R S
```

94

Look at this asswipe! See if you can find his shadow.

Answer on page 114

Math Squares

Answer on page 114

Try to fill in the missing numbers!

Use the numbers 1 to 9 to complete the equations and can be used more than once. Not good at math? You're fucked.

Each row is a math equation. Good luck with that shit. Work it in order of operations.

That's not all! Each column is a math equation, too. Surprise, bitch! Also order of operations.

2	x		+	4	/		6
+		x		/		x	
	-	5	x		+	4	5
-		+		-		/	
1	+		x	3	+		36
x		/		-		x	
	x	4	+		/	9	4
49		11		-7		18	

Here are the damn rules of a cryptogram:

You are given a fucked piece of text where each letter is substituted with a irrelevant damn number and you need to fucking decide which letter in the native alphabet is being coded by the numbers you are given.

You need to use logic and knowledge of the letters and words of our goddamn language to crack this shit or your fucked.

Answer on page 114

A	B	C	D	E	F	G	H	I

J	K	L	M	N	O	P	Q	R
						3		

S	T	U	V	W	X	Y	Z

__ '   __ | __ __   __ __ __ __
12   2   25   22 12 7 1

p
__ __ __ __ __ __ ,   __ __   __ __
3   1 20 19 16 22   19 16   12 9

__ ' __ | __ __ | __ __ __ __ __ __ __
12   2   25 22   25 19 19 14 16 23 1

    __ __   __ __ __ ,   __ __ __
    15 16   10 16 26   10 16 26

__ __ __ __ | __ __ | __ __ __ |
22 1 1 5   15 16   25 19 18

                                            ?
__ __ __ __ __ __ __ __   __ __ __ __
10 16 26 20 19 1 23 9   6 14 10

97

Ever play Sudoku? I bet you fucking haven't! Answer on page 114
These are the wanked rules.

Numbers from 1 to 9 are inserted into sets that have 9 x 9 = 81 squares in whole. Every number can be used just once in every, 3x3 block, column and row, so don't reuse the goddamn shit.

* Every number can be used just once in the blocks of 3 x 3 = 9 square blocks. Use a number more than once, your fucked.
* Each row of 9 numbers must fucking contain all digits 1 through 9 in any order, so don't fucking miss that shit.
* Every column of 9 numbers should comprise all digits 1 through 9 in any order. Hope you can fucking count, bitch.

Here's a hint for your stupid ass: One way to figure out which numbers can go in each space is to use "process of elimination" by checking to see which other numbers are already included within each square – remember, no duplicates.

				1				9
		6	8	4				
4	1	2			6		8	
7					8	5	3	
2								8
	6	8	3					4
	8		9			6	4	2
				8	4	9		
9				5				

Start at the top and work your way the fuck down to
the bottom of each finger!

Answer on page
114

Number Blocks

Answer on page 114

Are you smart enough to fill in the missing numbers?
The missing numbers are integers (that means it's a
whole number) from 0 to 9.
The numbers in each row add up to the totals to the
right.
The numbers in each column add up to the totals along
the bottom. Numbers can be repeated, so don't get
fucked and don't be an ass!
The diagonal lines also add up the totals to the right.
Good fucking luck!

					26
	3	5			18
3	7		7	0	19
4		0	8		22
	5			8	28
8		2		9	34
18	28	18	31	26	21

Check out these other fun fucking items by the Author:

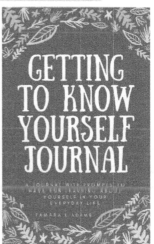

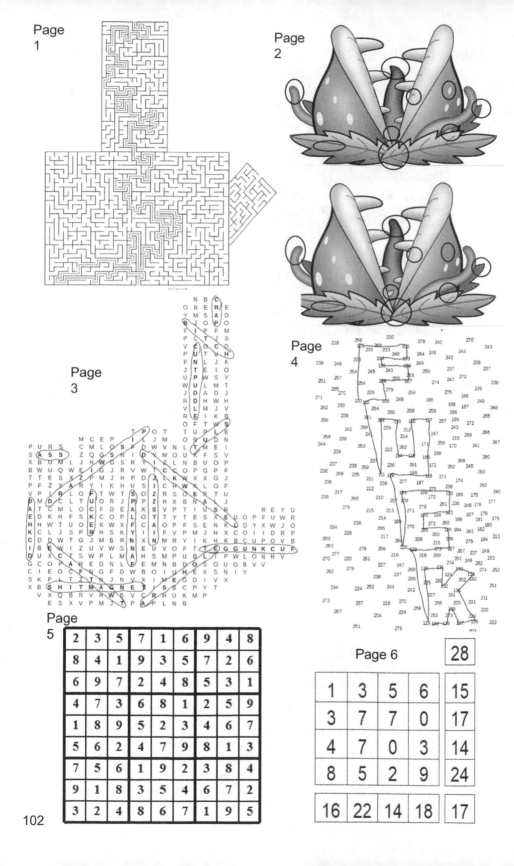

Page 1

Page 2

Page 3

Page 4

Page 5

2	3	5	7	1	6	9	4	8
8	4	1	9	3	5	7	2	6
6	9	7	2	4	8	5	3	1
4	7	3	6	8	1	2	5	9
1	8	9	5	2	3	4	6	7
5	6	2	4	7	9	8	1	3
7	5	6	1	9	2	3	8	4
9	1	8	3	5	4	6	7	2
3	2	4	8	6	7	1	9	5

Page 6

				28
1	3	5	6	15
3	7	7	0	17
4	7	0	3	14
8	5	2	9	24
16	22	14	18	17

102

Page 7

Just
shut
your
fucking
Mouth.
I
don't
take
any
shit
ever
and
I'm
not
doing
shit
today.

Page 8

I'm sorry I hurt your
feelings when I called
you stupid I really
though you
already knew.

Page 9

164

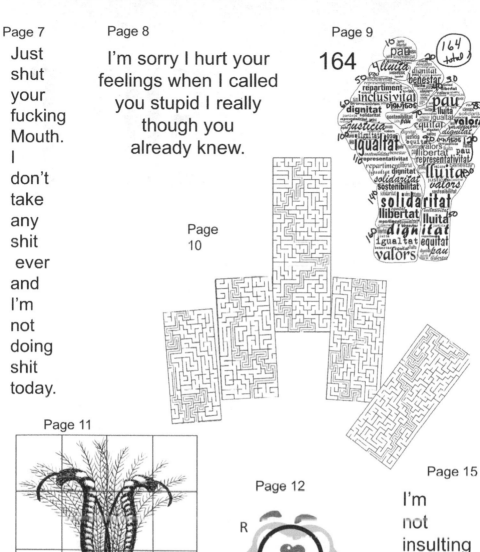

164
total

Page
10

Page 11

Page 12

R

Page 15

I'm
not
insulting
you.
I'm
describing
you.
You
miserable
piece
of
shit
for
brains.

Page 13

I never realize
how much I
swear until I'm in
a situation
where I can't.

Page 14

Sometimes only
bad words can
fully express your
feelings.

Page 25

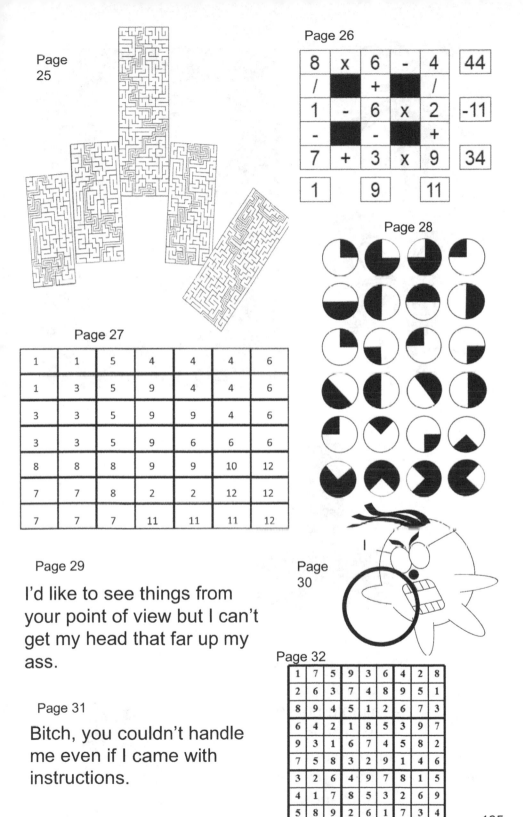

Page 26

8	x	6	-	4		44
/	■	+	■	/		
1	-	6	x	2		-11
-	■		-	+		
7	+	3	x	9		34

1		9		11

Page 28

Page 27

1	1	5	4	4	4	6
1	3	5	9	4	4	6
3	3	5	9	9	4	6
3	3	5	9	6	6	6
8	8	8	9	9	10	12
7	7	8	2	2	12	12
7	7	7	11	11	11	12

Page 29

I'd like to see things from your point of view but I can't get my head that far up my ass.

Page 30

Page 31

Bitch, you couldn't handle me even if I came with instructions.

Page 32

1	7	5	9	3	6	4	2	8
2	6	3	7	4	8	9	5	1
8	9	4	5	1	2	6	7	3
6	4	2	1	8	5	3	9	7
9	3	1	6	7	4	5	8	2
7	5	8	3	2	9	1	4	6
3	2	6	4	9	7	8	1	5
4	1	7	8	5	3	2	6	9
5	8	9	2	6	1	7	3	4

857
Total

Yes,
I
can.
now
get
the
fuck
out
of
my
way.
I
run
on
caffeine,
chaos,
and
cuss
words.

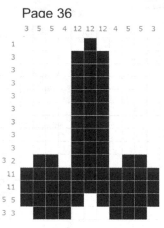

Some days, the
supply of
available curse
words is
insufficient to
meet my
demands

Page
40

Page 41

Page 42

Page 43

Page 44

2	8	3	9	6	28
2	0	5	9	3	19
1	3	7	0	4	15
5	9	3	6	2	25
8	5	3	6	8	30
18	25	21	30	23	23

39

Page 45

Page 46

8	7	5	2	1	3	4	6	9
3	9	6	8	4	7	1	2	5
4	1	2	5	9	6	3	8	7
7	4	9	1	2	8	5	3	6
2	5	3	4	6	9	7	1	8
1	6	8	3	7	5	2	9	4
5	8	7	9	3	1	6	4	2
6	2	1	7	8	4	9	5	3
9	3	4	6	5	2	8	7	1

Page 47

M

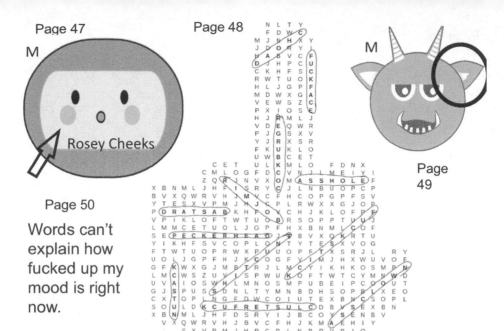

Rosey Cheeks

Page 48

Page 49

M

Page 50

Words can't explain how fucked up my mood is right now.

Page 51

9	x	3	-	7	20
/		+		-	
3	-	4	x	12	-45
-		/		+	
8	+	2	x	9	26

-5	5	4

Page 52

Page 53

3	9	5	7	4	6	2	8	1
6	7	1	9	8	2	3	4	5
8	2	4	3	1	5	9	7	6
2	3	9	1	5	7	8	6	4
5	4	8	2	6	3	1	9	7
1	6	7	4	9	8	5	2	3
4	1	2	6	3	9	7	5	8
7	5	3	8	2	4	6	1	9
9	8	6	5	7	1	4	3	2

I could eat a bowl of alphabet soup and shit out a smarter statement than that.

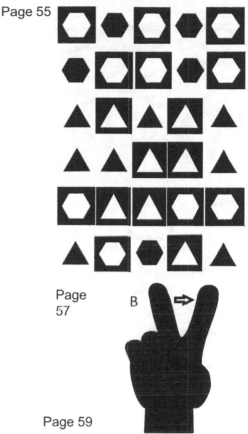

B

If you don't like me, take a map, get a car, drive to hell. Have a nice trip.

Hey auto correct, quit tampering with my curse words, you mother forklift.

Page 63

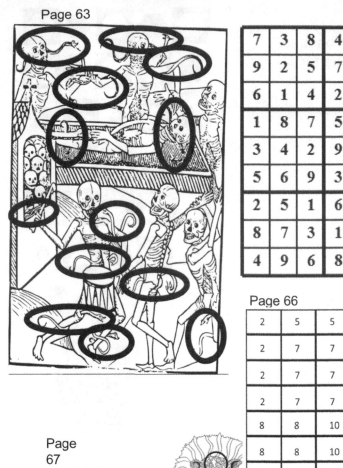

Page 65

7	3	8	4	1	9	2	6	5
9	2	5	7	8	6	1	4	3
6	1	4	2	3	5	8	7	9
1	8	7	5	6	2	9	3	4
3	4	2	9	7	1	6	5	8
5	6	9	3	4	8	7	2	1
2	5	1	6	9	3	4	8	7
8	7	3	1	2	4	5	9	6
4	9	6	8	5	7	3	1	2

Page 66

2	5	5	5	1	1	1
2	7	7	3	3	1	1
2	7	7	7	3	9	1
2	7	7	3	3	9	9
8	8	10	10	10	9	4
8	8	10	4	4	4	4
8	8	6	6	6	6	6

Page 67

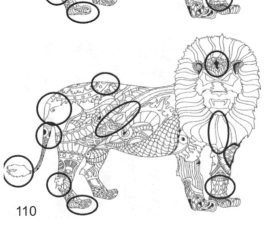

Page 68

110

Page 69

						36
7	2	6	9	4	0	28
3	1	9	2	4	8	27
4	5	6	8	2	7	32
2	4	8	2	6	0	22
1	8	5	9	5	6	34
8	5	3	0	3	9	28
25	25	37	30	24	30	30

Page 70

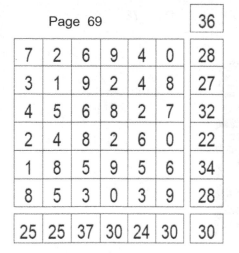

Page 71

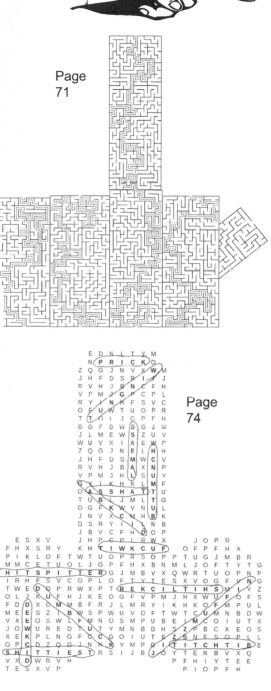

Page 72

What's the big deal? It
doesn't hurt anybody.
Fuck, fuckity, fuck-fuck-fuck!

Page 73

7	5	2	4	9	6	1	3	8
3	9	1	2	5	8	4	6	7
4	8	6	7	3	1	9	5	2
8	3	9	6	7	5	2	1	4
1	2	4	9	8	3	5	7	6
6	7	5	1	4	2	8	9	3
5	4	7	3	2	9	6	8	1
2	6	8	5	1	7	3	4	9
9	1	3	8	6	4	7	2	5

Page 74

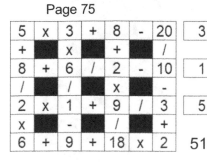

Page 75

5	x	3	+	8	-	20	3
+		x		+		/	
8	+	6	/	2	-	10	1
/		/		x		-	
2	x	1	+	9	/	3	5
x		-		/		+	
6	+	9	+	18	x	2	51

29		9		9		1

111

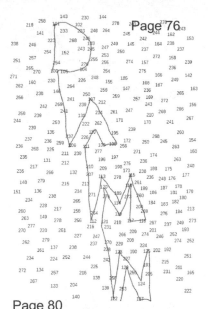

G

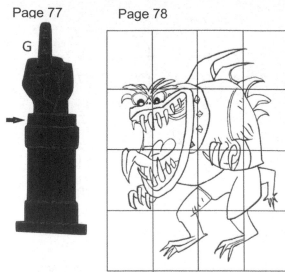

Page 79

I don't know about you, but people make me want to say bad words.

Page 81

If you don't want a sarcastic answer, don't ask a stupid question.

Page 80

7	5	2	4	9	6	1	3	8
3	9	1	2	5	8	4	6	7
4	8	6	7	3	1	9	5	2
8	3	9	6	7	5	2	1	4
1	2	4	9	8	3	5	7	6
6	7	5	1	4	2	8	9	3
5	4	7	3	2	9	6	8	1
2	6	8	5	1	7	3	4	9
9	1	3	8	6	4	7	2	5

You're such a nutsack
Fuck this chisel
Get moving Bitches
Bitches get shit done
Fuck me!
Bloody Hell
Fuck Shit Up!
Suck my balls
Holy shitballs
A metric fuck-ton
Fuck me Sideways
Mother-shit-fuck!
Go shit up a rope
What the actual fuck!
Fucking Bunch of Idiots

Page 82

Page 83

Page 84

S   Hearts for eyes

Page 85

						38
1	3	5	3	2	6	20
3	7	2	7	5	0	24
4	8	0	8	7	3	30
2	5	9	4	9	8	37
6	2	1	5	0	4	18
8	6	2	9	3	9	37
24	31	19	36	26	30	21

Page 86

Dear auto correct, stop correcting my swear words you piece of shut.

66
Assholes.

Page 88

Page 89

J

Page 92

Page 91

Page 93

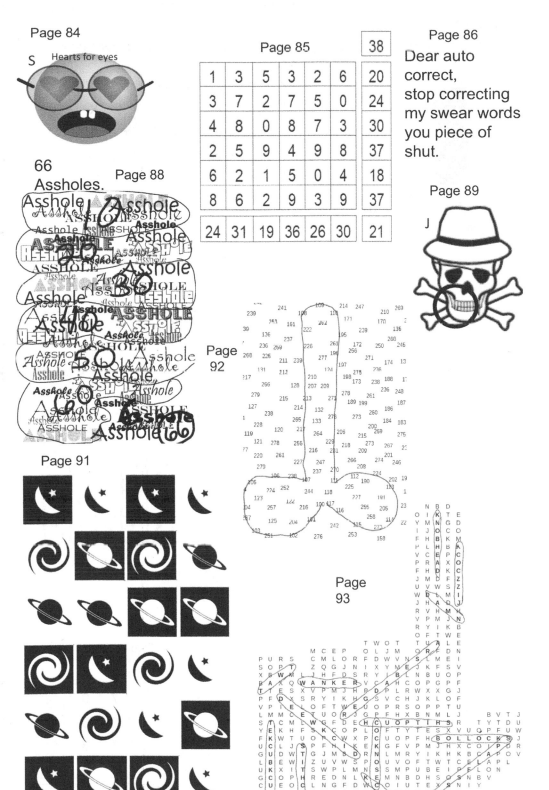

113

Books by Tamara L Adams

F*ck I'm Bored
Angry Journal
Art Up This Journal
Activititties
Activity Book for Adults
Activity Book You Never Knew You Wanted But Can't Live Without
Activity Book You need to Buy Before You Die
Fuck I'm Bored : Adult Activity Book
The Activity Book That Will Transform Your Life
Activities to do while you number two
Timmy and the Dragon
Pebble pal pete
Unmotivated Coloring
Angry Coloring
Coloring Happy Quotes
Inspirational Quotes Coloring
Coloring Cocktails
Cussing Creatures Color
101 Quote Inspired Journal Prompts
76 Quote Inspired Journal Prompts
51 Quote Inspired Journal Prompts
Unlocking Happiness Planner
Daily Fitness Planner
Bloggers Daily Planner
Bloggers Daily Planner w margins
Writers Daily Planner
Writers Daily Planner w coloring
Busy Mothers Planner
Where's Woody Coloring Book
M.A.S.H.
99 Writing Prompts
Deciding Destiny: Christy's Choice
Deciding Destiny: Matt's Choice
Deciding Destiny: Lindsays Choice
Deciding Destiny: Joe's Choice
Rich Stryker: Julie's Last Hope
Rich Stryker: Tom's Final Justice
Unlocking Happiness
Getting to Know Yourself Journal
#2 Getting to Know Yourself Journal

Thanks for your goddman purchase!!

Please leave a review! I would be fucking grateful.

Contact me to get a free printable PDF of activities at:
http://www.tamaraladamsauthor.com/free-printable-activity-book-pdf/

.

Tamaraadamsauthor@gmail.com

Thank you for your support and have a great fucking day!

You can contact me at

http://www.amazon.com/T.L.-Adams/e/B00YSROGC4

Tammy@tamaraladamsauthor.com

https://www.pinterest.com/Tjandlexismom/

https://twitter.com/TamaraLAdams

https://www.facebook.com/TamaraLAdamsAuthor/

https://www.youtube.com/user/tamaraladams

https://www.instagram.com/tamaraladamsauthor/

http://www.tamaraladamsauthor.com

Made in the USA
Monee, IL
06 May 2022

96011547R00069